The Journey of John Fetterman

A Progressive Trailblazer's Rise from Revitalizing Rust Belt Towns to National Political Stage

Terry L. Neil

Copyright © 2024 Terry L. Neil

All rights reserved. No part of this publication may be reproduced, distributed, or transmitted in any form or by any means, including photocopying, recording, or other electronic or mechanical methods, without the prior written permission of the publisher, except in the case of brief quotations embodied in critical reviews and certain other noncommercial uses permitted by copyright law

Table Of Contents

Introduction

Chapter 1

Mayor of Braddock

Chapter 2

Lieutenant Governor of Pennsylvania

Chapter 3

U.S. Senate Campaigns

Chapter 4

Senate Tenure and Challenges

Chapter 5

Political Positions and Advocacy

Chapter 6

Personal Life and Impact

Conclusion

Introduction

- Setting the Stage: Early Life and Education
  - The Call to Public Service: Fetterman's Journey Begins

Introduction

John Fetterman's rise in American politics is nothing short of remarkable. From his humble beginnings to his current position as a United States Senator, Fetterman's journey is characterized by a commitment to progressive values, innovative leadership, and resilience in the face of challenges. This biography seeks to explore the various facets of Fetterman's life and career, shedding light on the key moments and decisions that have shaped his trajectory.

Setting the Stage: Early Life and Education

John Karl Fetterman was born on August 15, 1969, in West Reading, Pennsylvania. Growing up in the suburbs of Pittsburgh, Fetterman was exposed to both the struggles of working-class communities and the opportunities that education could provide. Despite facing economic hardship, Fetterman excelled academically and demonstrated a keen interest in social justice from a young age.

Fetterman pursued higher education at Albright College, where he studied finance and earned his bachelor's degree. It was during this time that he began to develop a deeper understanding of socioeconomic inequality and the role of public policy in addressing systemic issues. After completing his undergraduate studies, Fetterman furthered his education at the University of Connecticut, where he obtained a Master of Business Administration (MBA) degree.

However, it was Fetterman's experiences beyond the classroom that would ultimately shape his worldview and ignite his passion for public service. Following his graduate studies, Fetterman embarked on a transformative journey with AmeriCorps, a national service program aimed at addressing critical community needs. It was during his time with AmeriCorps that Fetterman first set foot in Braddock, Pennsylvania, a once-thriving steel town that had fallen on hard times following the collapse of the steel industry.

The Call to Public Service: Fetterman's Journey Begins

In 2004, Fetterman made the fateful decision to move to Braddock permanently, drawn by a desire to make a tangible difference in the lives of its residents. Just one year later, in 2005, he was elected as the mayor of Braddock, marking the beginning of his political career. As mayor, Fetterman quickly gained a reputation for his unconventional approach to revitalizing the struggling town, eschewing traditional methods in favor of innovative solutions.

Fetterman's tenure as mayor was characterized by a relentless focus on addressing the root causes of poverty and inequality. He spearheaded initiatives aimed at promoting economic development, investing in education and youth programs, and harnessing the power of art and culture to revitalize Braddock's economy. Through his bold leadership and hands-on approach, Fetterman transformed Braddock into a symbol of resilience and hope, garnering national attention in the process.

It was during his time as mayor that Fetterman's commitment to progressive values and social justice became increasingly evident. He advocated for healthcare as a fundamental right, championed criminal justice reform, and fought tirelessly to uplift marginalized communities. Fetterman's success in Braddock laid the foundation for his subsequent political career, propelling him onto the national stage as a leading voice for change.

Chapter 1: Mayor of Braddock

When John Fetterman assumed the role of mayor of Braddock in 2005, he inherited a town grappling with decades of economic decline and urban decay. Once a thriving hub of steel production, Braddock had fallen on hard times following the collapse of the steel industry in the 1980s. The town's population had dwindled, businesses had shuttered, and infrastructure had deteriorated, leaving behind a landscape of vacant lots and abandoned buildings.

Despite these challenges, Fetterman saw potential in Braddock where others saw despair. He recognized the resilience of its residents and the rich history that permeated its streets. Fetterman's vision for Braddock was not just about revitalizing its economy; it was about restoring hope and dignity to a community that had been forgotten by many.

At the heart of Fetterman's vision for revitalizing Braddock was a commitment to inclusive and sustainable development. Rather than relying solely on traditional economic models, Fetterman sought to leverage the town's assets and empower its residents to drive change from within. He believed that Braddock's future lay in embracing its past while embracing innovation and creativity.

Fetterman prioritized initiatives that would create opportunities for economic growth while also addressing the social and cultural needs of the community. He worked to attract new businesses and investment to Braddock, revitalizing its commercial corridors and creating job opportunities for residents. At the same time, Fetterman recognized the importance of investing in education, healthcare, and social services to ensure that all residents could benefit from the town's resurgence.

One of the most distinctive aspects of Fetterman's approach to revitalization was his embrace of art and culture as catalysts for change. Recognizing the power of creativity to inspire, unite, and transform, Fetterman launched a series of initiatives aimed at integrating art into the fabric of Braddock's community.

Under Fetterman's leadership, Braddock became home to an array of artistic endeavors, including public art installations, community murals, and cultural events. These initiatives not only beautified the town but also fostered a sense of pride and belonging among residents. Moreover, they attracted visitors from across the region, helping to put Braddock back on the map as a destination for creativity and innovation.

In addition to promoting the arts, Fetterman prioritized investments in youth programs and education. He recognized that the future of Braddock depended on its young people and sought to provide them with the resources and opportunities they needed to succeed. Fetterman spearheaded initiatives to expand access to quality education, support after-school programs, and create safe spaces for children and teenagers to learn and grow.

As Fetterman's revitalization efforts gained momentum, they began to attract attention from beyond the borders of Braddock. His innovative approach to governance and commitment to social justice resonated with people across the country, earning him recognition as a rising star in American politics.

Fetterman's leadership in Braddock was characterized by a willingness to think outside the box and take bold risks in pursuit of his vision. Whether it was converting abandoned buildings into community centers, partnering with artists to transform vacant lots into vibrant public spaces, or advocating for progressive policies at the state and national levels, Fetterman was unafraid to challenge the status quo and push the boundaries of what was possible.

As a result, Fetterman became a sought-after speaker and commentator, sharing his insights and experiences with audiences far and wide. His TED Talk, "The Power of One: Reinventing America's Small Towns," garnered millions of views and further elevated his profile as a thought leader in community development. In 2016, Fetterman gained national attention when he ran for the United States Senate, bringing his message of hope, resilience, and inclusive leadership to the forefront of American politics.

Chapter 2: Lieutenant Governor of Pennsylvania

After making a name for himself as the mayor of Braddock, John Fetterman set his sights on higher office, running for lieutenant governor of Pennsylvania in 2018. His decision to enter state politics marked a new chapter in his career, one that would see him continue his advocacy for progressive policies on a larger stage.

From the outset of his tenure as lieutenant governor, Fetterman wasted no time in championing a bold agenda centered on issues such as healthcare, education, criminal justice reform, and economic equality. Drawing on his experiences in

Braddock, he sought to bring attention to the plight of struggling communities across Pennsylvania and to advocate for policies that would uplift the most vulnerable.

Fetterman's approach to governance was characterized by a commitment to transparency, accessibility, and grassroots engagement. He traveled extensively throughout the state, holding town hall meetings in every county to listen to the concerns of Pennsylvanians and to ensure that their voices were heard in Harrisburg. This hands-on approach to leadership earned Fetterman praise for his accessibility and responsiveness to the needs of constituents.

One of the key issues that Fetterman championed during his tenure as lieutenant governor was the legalization of cannabis for both medical and recreational use. Recognizing the economic potential of the cannabis industry and the social justice implications of prohibition, Fetterman became a vocal advocate for legalization, arguing that it could generate much-needed revenue for the state while also addressing racial disparities in drug enforcement.

In addition to his advocacy for cannabis legalization, Fetterman emerged as a leading voice in the fight to protect the integrity of Pennsylvania's elections. In the wake of baseless claims of voter fraud and efforts to suppress voting rights, Fetterman spoke out forcefully in defense of democracy, calling for measures to expand access to voting and to ensure that every eligible voter could cast their ballot safely and securely.

During his term as lieutenant governor, Fetterman faced a number of challenges, both political and personal. As a progressive voice in a state government controlled by Republicans, he often found himself at odds with the legislative majority on issues ranging from healthcare to gun control. Despite these obstacles, Fetterman remained undeterred in his efforts to advance his agenda and to fight for the people of Pennsylvania.

One of the defining moments of Fetterman's tenure came in 2019 when he defied a directive from the Republican-controlled state Senate to remove his Black Lives Matter flag from the balcony of his office at the Capitol. In a show of solidarity with the movement for racial justice, Fetterman refused to back down, sparking a debate about free speech and the role of public officials in addressing systemic racism.

Despite the challenges he faced, Fetterman also achieved notable successes during his time as lieutenant governor. He played a key role in the passage of legislation to expand access to healthcare for low-income Pennsylvanians, fought to raise the minimum wage, and advocated for criminal justice reforms aimed at reducing mass incarceration and addressing racial disparities in the justice system. Through his bold leadership and unwavering commitment to progressive values, Fetterman left an indelible mark on Pennsylvania politics and emerged as a leading voice for change in the state.

Chapter 3: U.S. Senate Campaigns

John Fetterman's journey to the U.S. Senate began with his first campaign in 2016. Running as a Democratic candidate in the primary election, Fetterman sought to establish himself as a champion for working-class Pennsylvanians and a voice for progressive change. Drawing on his experiences as mayor of Braddock, Fetterman campaigned on a platform focused on economic revitalization, social justice, and environmental sustainability.

Throughout the campaign, Fetterman emphasized the need to address income inequality, create good-paying jobs, and invest in infrastructure and education to uplift struggling communities across Pennsylvania. He also spoke out against corporate interests and the influence of money in politics, positioning himself as a grassroots candidate committed to fighting for the interests of ordinary citizens.

While Fetterman ultimately fell short in the primary election, finishing third behind Katie McGinty and Joe Sestak, his campaign laid the groundwork for his future political endeavors and helped to elevate his profile on the national stage.

Following his Senate run in 2016, Fetterman turned his attention to the race for lieutenant governor of Pennsylvania in 2018. Drawing on the momentum generated by his previous campaign, Fetterman launched a spirited bid for the Democratic nomination, running on a platform focused on economic justice, criminal justice reform, and healthcare.

Throughout the campaign, Fetterman traveled the state, meeting with voters in communities large and small and listening to their concerns. He emphasized the importance of building a diverse coalition of supporters and reaching out to traditionally marginalized groups, including people of color, LGBTQ+ individuals, and working-class voters.

Fetterman's message resonated with voters across Pennsylvania, and he emerged victorious in a crowded primary field, securing the Democratic nomination for lieutenant governor. In the general election, he went on to defeat his Republican opponent, Jeff Bartos, by a comfortable margin, becoming the first Democrat to hold the office in over a decade.

In 2022, John Fetterman embarked on his most ambitious political campaign yet, launching a bid for the U.S. Senate seat being vacated by retiring Senator Pat Toomey. Running in a crowded Democratic primary field that included several well-funded opponents, Fetterman once again positioned himself as a champion for progressive values and a voice for change.

Throughout the primary campaign, Fetterman focused on issues such as healthcare, climate change, and economic inequality, rallying support from grassroots activists, labor unions, and progressive organizations. He also emphasized his track record as lieutenant governor, highlighting his efforts to expand access to healthcare, advocate for criminal justice reform, and fight for working families.

Despite facing fierce competition from fellow Democrats, Fetterman emerged victorious in the primary election, winning a hard-fought battle for the party's nomination. In the general election, he faced off against Republican nominee Mehmet Oz, a celebrity doctor with ties to former President Donald Trump.

Throughout the general election campaign, Fetterman continued to champion his progressive platform, contrasting his record of public service with Oz's lack of political experience and highlighting the stakes of the election for Pennsylvanians. Despite being outspent by his opponent, Fetterman ran a disciplined and focused campaign, emphasizing his commitment to fighting for the interests of working-class families and advancing progressive policies in Washington.

On election day, Fetterman emerged victorious, defeating Oz by a comfortable margin and securing a seat in the U.S. Senate. His victory marked the culmination of years of hard work and dedication to public service, and it positioned him as a rising star in the Democratic Party with a bright future ahead.

Chapter 4: Senate Tenure and Challenges

John Fetterman's entry into the U.S. Senate marked a significant milestone in his political career. Sworn in as Pennsylvania's junior senator, Fetterman brought with him a wealth of experience gained from his tenure as mayor of Braddock and lieutenant governor of Pennsylvania. As he settled into his new role in Washington, Fetterman wasted no time in getting to work on behalf of the people of his state.

From the outset, Fetterman made it clear that he would be a vocal advocate for progressive policies and a forceful critic of the status quo. He quickly established himself as a leading voice on issues such as healthcare, economic inequality, and criminal justice reform, drawing on his firsthand experiences and the stories of the people he had met during his time in public service.

However, Fetterman's early days in the Senate were not without their challenges. Shortly after taking office, he faced a personal health crisis that threatened to derail his nascent Senate career.

In the midst of his first term in the Senate, John Fetterman was diagnosed with a serious medical condition that required immediate treatment. The news came as a shock to Fetterman and his family, but true to form, he faced the challenge head-on with characteristic courage and determination.

Despite the physical toll of his illness and the demands of his Senate duties, Fetterman refused to let his health struggles define him. With the support of his loved ones and the medical care he needed, he embarked on a course of treatment that would ultimately lead to his recovery.

Throughout his battle with illness, Fetterman remained focused on his responsibilities as a senator and continued to fight for the causes he believed in. He attended hearings, met with constituents, and participated in debates, all while undergoing treatment and recuperating from surgery.

Fetterman's resilience in the face of adversity served as an inspiration to many, demonstrating his unwavering commitment to public service and his determination to overcome any obstacle in the pursuit of a better future for all Pennsylvanians.

As a member of the U.S. Senate, John Fetterman wasted no time in making his mark on Capitol Hill. From the outset, he made it clear that he would be a tireless advocate for the people of Pennsylvania, fighting for their interests and championing progressive policies.

One of Fetterman's top legislative priorities was healthcare reform. Drawing on his experiences as lieutenant governor, where he had worked to expand access to healthcare for all Pennsylvanians, Fetterman pushed for measures to lower prescription drug costs, protect coverage for pre-existing conditions, and expand access to affordable care.

In addition to healthcare, Fetterman also focused on issues such as economic inequality, climate change, and criminal justice reform. He sponsored legislation to raise the minimum wage, invest in renewable energy, and reform the criminal justice system, drawing on his experiences as mayor of Braddock and his commitment to social justice.

In recognition of his leadership and expertise, Fetterman was appointed to several key committees in the Senate, including the Committee on Health, Education, Labor, and Pensions; the Committee on Banking, Housing, and Urban Affairs; and the Committee on Environment and Public Works. These committee assignments allowed Fetterman to play a leading role in shaping legislation on a wide range of issues and to advocate for the priorities of the people of Pennsylvania at the highest levels of government.

Chapter 5: Political Positions and Advocacy

Throughout his career in public service, John Fetterman has been a vocal advocate for progressive policies and a champion of social justice. From his early days as mayor of Braddock to his tenure as lieutenant governor of Pennsylvania and his current role as a U.S. senator, Fetterman has consistently fought for the rights of marginalized communities and the interests of working-class Americans.

Healthcare reform has been a cornerstone of Fetterman's political agenda since the beginning of his career. As mayor of Braddock, he witnessed firsthand the devastating impact of lack of access to healthcare on low-income communities. In response, he worked to expand healthcare services in Braddock and fought for policies to ensure that all Pennsylvanians have access to affordable, quality healthcare.

In the Senate, Fetterman has continued to advocate for healthcare reform, sponsoring legislation to lower prescription drug costs, protect coverage for pre-existing conditions, and expand access to Medicaid. He has also been a vocal supporter of a Medicare for All system, arguing that healthcare should be a fundamental right for all Americans, not a privilege reserved for the wealthy.

Criminal justice reform is another issue that Fetterman is passionate about. As mayor of

Braddock, he worked to implement innovative programs to reduce crime and address the root causes of violence, such as poverty and lack of economic opportunity. In the Senate, he has continued to push for reforms to the criminal justice system, including ending mass incarceration, reforming sentencing laws, and investing in alternatives to incarceration such as drug treatment and mental health services.

Environmental policy is another area where Fetterman has been a strong advocate for progressive change. He has been a vocal supporter of renewable energy and has called for bold action to address climate change, including transitioning to a clean energy economy and investing in green infrastructure. He has also been a critic of the fossil fuel industry and has called for stronger regulations to protect the environment and public health.

Fetterman has been a vocal advocate for immigration reform throughout his political career. He believes that the United States has a moral obligation to provide a pathway to citizenship for undocumented immigrants who have lived and worked in the country for years, and he has called for comprehensive immigration reform that includes a path to citizenship, border security, and protections for Dreamers.

In addition to immigration reform, Fetterman has been a strong advocate for social justice and civil rights. He has spoken out against discrimination and bigotry in all its forms and has been a vocal supporter of the Black Lives Matter movement. He has also called for reforms to address systemic racism in areas such as education, healthcare, and criminal justice.

On the international stage, Fetterman has taken positions on a range of foreign policy issues, from the Israeli-Palestinian conflict to relations with China and Russia. He has been a vocal critic of Israel's treatment of Palestinians and has called for a more even-handed approach to the conflict that respects the rights and dignity of both Israelis and Palestinians.

In regards to China, Fetterman has been a vocal critic of the Chinese government's human rights abuses and authoritarian policies. He has called for stronger action to hold China accountable for its violations of human rights and has advocated for measures to protect American workers and businesses from unfair trade practices.

In regards to Ukraine, Fetterman has been a staunch supporter of Ukraine's sovereignty and territorial integrity in the face of Russian aggression. He has called for increased military aid to Ukraine and has supported sanctions against Russia for its actions in Crimea and eastern Ukraine. He has also called for stronger diplomatic efforts to resolve the conflict and promote peace and stability in the region.

Overall, Fetterman's foreign policy stances reflect his commitment to human rights, democracy, and international cooperation. He believes that the United States has a responsibility to stand up for the rights of oppressed people around the world and to promote peace and stability through diplomacy and engagement.

Chapter 6: Personal Life and Impact

Beyond his political career, John Fetterman's personal life has been marked by significant events and influences that have shaped both him and his trajectory in public service. From his relationship with his wife, Gisele Barreto Fetterman, to his resilience in the face of health challenges, Fetterman's personal journey has played a central role in defining his impact on American politics.

Gisele Barreto Fetterman, John Fetterman's wife, has been a powerful influence on his life and career. Born in Brazil, Gisele immigrated to the United States as a child and grew up in poverty in New York City. Her experiences as an immigrant and as a survivor of domestic violence have deeply influenced her worldview and her commitment to social justice.

John and Gisele met while they were both students at Harvard University, where they bonded over their shared commitment to public service and social activism. After graduating, they moved to Braddock, Pennsylvania, where John became mayor and Gisele became actively involved in community organizing and advocacy.

As Pennsylvania's Second Lady during John's tenure as lieutenant governor, Gisele used her platform to advocate for immigrant rights, women's rights, and criminal justice reform. She founded the Free Store in Braddock, a nonprofit organization that provides essential goods and services to families in need, and she has been a vocal advocate for policies to address poverty and inequality in Pennsylvania.

Gisele's influence on John's political career has been profound. Her passion for social justice and her commitment to serving others have inspired and motivated him to fight for progressive change and to use his position of power to uplift marginalized communities.

Throughout his life, John Fetterman has faced numerous health challenges that have tested his resilience and determination. In 2001, he was diagnosed with a rare form of bone cancer called desmoid tumor, which required extensive surgery and treatment. Despite the physical and emotional toll of his illness, Fetterman remained committed to his work as mayor of Braddock and continued to advocate for his community.

In 2008, Fetterman faced another health scare when he suffered a heart attack at the age of 38. The experience forced him to confront his own mortality and led him to reevaluate his priorities in life. He became even more determined to make a difference in the world and to fight for the issues he believed in.

Fetterman's journey to recovery has been marked by resilience, courage, and a deep appreciation for life. He credits his wife,

Gisele, and his family for their unwavering support during his darkest moments, and he is grateful for the second chance at life that he has been given.

As John Fetterman's political career continues to evolve, his impact on American politics looms large. From his early days as mayor of Braddock to his current role as a U.S. senator, Fetterman has been a tireless advocate for progressive change and a voice for the voiceless.

His innovative leadership in Braddock, his advocacy for healthcare reform and criminal justice reform, and his commitment to social justice and equality have earned him a devoted following and have solidified his place as a rising star in the Democratic Party.

Looking ahead, Fetterman's future prospects in American politics seem bright. With his unapologetically progressive agenda and his ability to connect with voters across party lines, he has the potential to make a significant impact on the national stage.

Whether he continues to serve in the Senate, runs for higher office, or pursues other avenues of public service, one thing is clear: John Fetterman's legacy as a champion for the people will endure for years to come.

Conclusion

As we reflect on John Fetterman's remarkable political journey, it becomes clear that his impact extends far beyond the boundaries of Pennsylvania. From his humble beginnings in Braddock to his current role as a U.S. senator, Fetterman has emerged as a bold and unapologetic voice for progressive change in American politics.

Fetterman's journey began in the struggling steel town of Braddock, where he served as mayor for over a decade. In Braddock, Fetterman gained national attention for his innovative approach to revitalizing the town, which included initiatives focused on art, youth programs, and community engagement. His leadership in Braddock laid the groundwork for his future political career and earned him a reputation as a fearless advocate for the underprivileged.

Fetterman's tenure as lieutenant governor of Pennsylvania further solidified his status as a rising star in the Democratic Party. During his time in office, he championed progressive policies on issues ranging from healthcare and criminal justice reform to cannabis legalization and election integrity. His willingness to take on controversial issues and his ability to connect with voters across the political spectrum made him a formidable force in Pennsylvania politics.

In 2022, Fetterman's political journey reached new heights when he was elected to the U.S. Senate, becoming one of the few openly progressive senators in Congress. His victory in the Senate race was a testament to his grassroots organizing efforts and his ability to inspire a diverse coalition of supporters.

As Fetterman looks to the future, he carries with him a wealth of lessons learned from his political journey. He understands the importance of grassroots organizing, coalition building, and staying true to one's principles in the face of adversity. He knows that change is not always easy, but it is worth fighting for, and he remains committed to his vision of a more just and equitable society.

Looking ahead, Fetterman's future in American politics seems bright. As a U.S. senator, he has the opportunity to shape national policy and be a voice for the voiceless on issues that matter most to everyday Americans. Whether he continues to champion progressive causes in the Senate, runs for higher office, or pursues other avenues of public service, one thing is certain: John Fetterman's impact on American politics will endure for generations to come.

In conclusion, John Fetterman's political journey is a testament to the power of perseverance, principle, and passion in the fight for a better world. As he continues to make his mark on the national stage, his legacy as a champion for the people will inspire future generations of leaders to follow in his footsteps.

Made in United States
Troutdale, OR
06/10/2024

20444902R00037